C000093467

'Oscar has identified the critical skill
executives need to lead effectively,
but which is often forgotten in a world
where our attention span is defined by
140 characters. Deep listening creates
trust and authentic action for leaders
at all levels and is crucial to the
development and retention of talent.
This is a highly valuable book.'

MARTIN MACKAY

President AsiaPacific, CA Technologies

'Oscar identifies the behaviours we
all need to practice to be effective
communicators, leaders and influencers –
it's the lost art of listening.'

DOMINIC PRICE

Head of R&D and Work Futurist, Atlassian

'Oscar's profound understanding of listening is so clearly demonstrated in this book. I had so many "aha!" moments. I realised I need to make more time to build a foundation for listening and embrace the pause moments because that is where you can really hear what another person is truly saying (and not saying!).'

JANE KING
Marketing Director, APN Outdoor

'Unlike our other senses, listening is collaborative. It's an act of sharing and a powerful means to create and reach different and more ambitious outcomes than those allowed by staying within our own thoughts. Oscar doesn't allow us to blame chatter and endless noise as reasons behind our choosing not to listen. He simply reminds us how, why and what might happen when we do listen deeply.'

JOHN KEITH
Managing Director and Head of Financial Institution Coverage, BNP Paribas

'Oscar consistently demonstrates the power in listening to what isn't being said – to those subtle silent moments between the stories, words, explanations, excuses and justifications. Really listening into these silent moments is when the clarity comes.'

TRACY HALL
Head of Brand and
Marketing Communications, eBay

'It's books like these that make you stop and think. Oscar does a brilliant job of challenging the way you traditionally think – about yourself, different situations and others – all with relevant and practical examples. It's a book I will certainly read over and over again. Highly recommended!'

SHARON LEWIS
Chief Marketing and Digital Officer, Future You

'As a self-confessed talker, learning the skill of deep listening has proved hard, but absolutely invaluable. It is the game changer that turned me from a manager into a leader. Shutting my mouth was only step one. Oscar's book pushed me to quieten my mind and really listen. It's transformed the way I communicate.'

PIA COYLE
Chief Investment Officer, Ikon Communications

'In today's "attention economy" of endless notifications and ubiquitous connectivity, the ability to choose where and when we expend our precious resource is more important than ever. Oscar's work recognises the impact of attention in creating connection and impact. This book provides valuable insights and simple techniques to begin our own journeys toward deep listening.'

TRACY MOORE
Director, KPMG

'The ability to listen is truly one of our greatest gifts – yet it's too often is overlooked in the pursuit of being heard. Oscar's concept of deep listening is well worth taking the time to listen to.'

ANDREW HOWIE
Group Marketing Manager,
Meat & Livestock Australia

'This book is a great reminder of just how important it is for leaders to stop trying to have all the answers all the time, and actually achieve the best collaborative outcomes through allowing everyone the chance to be heard. In an increasingly noisy world, the key to unlocking both personal and business growth, is to practice the art of listening.'

SIMON DAVENPORT
National Advertising and Communications Manager, Officeworks Ltd

'A key factor in achieving employee engagement is the ability to engage other people in conversation. That requires excellent listening skills, and Oscar manages to get around all critical aspects of this in *Deep Listening*. If you are too busy to listen, or are working with people who are, then this book can help you.
I say that because it helped me.'

CAI KJAER
CEO, SWOOP Analytics

'It's a tantalising concept to be able to turn off the distracting chatter we carry in our brains and allow ourselves to practise deep listening. Oscar eloquently outlines strategies to manage the struggle between feeling like we should be leading, when we would achieve more from listening. Relevant, practical and insightful – it will make you reconsider what listening actually is.'

LYNDALL SPOONER
Managing Director, 5th Dimension

'What struck me is that the ability to listen, to really listen, just needs you! There is real leadership strength in paying attention and responding appropriately.'

SHELLEY HUDSON
General Manager Organisational Effectiveness, TAL Limited

'All decision makers out there, listen up! This is the sound of change we've been longing to hear. Oscar clearly explains how listening between the noise can be a critical advantage.'

SÉRGIO BRODSKY
Head of Strategy, Initiative

'Oscar has identified the most powerful skill everybody needs in life and business. What really resonated with me were the five levels of listening ... brilliant.'

GREG GRAHAM
Group Marketing Director, WPP

'As a GM, board director, new father, team leader, manager, husband and son, it's sometimes hard to be fully present. The default solution is too often to try to cram more in, multi-task, move fast, talk faster and type simultaneously in an attempt to be "there" for everyone, cover all bases and to make quick decisions. Oscar challenges us to all reflect on whether instead we are unconsciously achieving the opposite – disengaged teams, duplication, missed information, avoidable mistakes – and the impact that may be having to, not just our people's lives but, our own health and fulfilment. Take a breath, read this book and start to re-learn the art of listening.'

PAUL CONNELL

Recovering Interrupting Listener, new father, General Manager and Marketing Director, Unilever

'In his own inimitable style, Oscar challenges conventional thinking and provides a common-sense approach to deep listening. He addresses the often-misplaced expectations and insecurities that leaders have, which drive the feeling that we need to do all the talking rather than use smart techniques to listen and engage to provide clarity and direction. This is what will lead to improved understanding, performance and engagement.'

ANDY MOFFAT
Chief People and Culture Officer, TAL Limited

'Epictetus told us that we have one mouth and two ears so that we can listen twice as much as we speak, yet most us need to be taught how to do this. Deep listening does this and more! You will uncover invaluable advice on how to listen effectively to what is being said, and, more importantly, what is unsaid. A must read for anyone wanting to be a better employee, leader, partner or friend.'

NICKI LUTHER
Senior HR Business Partner, Stryker

Deep Listening

Impact beyond words

Oscar Trimboli

ISBN: 978-0-9953777-4-5

Editing by Kelly Irving
kellyirving.com

Cover and internal layout by Ellie Schroeder
ellieschroeder.com

Illustrations by Presentation Studio
presentationstudio.com

oscartrimboli.com

Every human asks
to be *listened* to
– yet what they
crave most is
to be *heard*.

Contents

Preface

The world is a noisy place where you fight to be heard every day. Despite the fact that we have been taught at home and at school how to speak, none of us have had any training in *how to listen*. Multiple academic studies[1] have shown that between 50% and 55% of your working day is spent listening.

Our ability to broadcast messages has exponentially increased, yet it has dramatically reduced our ability to understand and communicate what is being said in a way that creates progress.

---

1 US Department of Labor – 1991 -55%. Werner – 1975 - 55%. Bohlken 1999 – 53%

We feel frustrated, isolated and confused because we aren't heard.

As a speaker, it takes absolutely no training to notice when someone isn't listening – they're distracted, they interrupt or drift away as you talk.

Yet the opposite is also true, without any training in how to listen we struggle to stay connected with the speaker and the discussion.

This results in unproductive workplaces where people fight to be heard and need to repeat themselves constantly, send emails to confirm what they said and then have follow-up meetings to ensure what was said was actually heard by those in the meeting. It's a downward spiral that drains energy from every conversation and reduces the productivity of organisations.

This is just one of many reasons I have created this guide.

Within these pages you will find an easy-to-access set of hacks and tips, for work and home, that will quickly move you from being an unconscious listener to someone who can listen *deeply* to what is said, and more importantly, someone who makes an impact by listening to what is *unsaid*.

AT THE END OF EACH CHAPTER

In the process of writing this guide, I asked many of you about your personal listening experiences and thoughts. I asked what makes a great listener, and what makes a poor listener, what are the costs of not listening and what are the benefits when you listen intently. Some of the survey responses to these questions are captured in grey (like this) at the end of each chapter. It is truly by listening to each other that we begin to create insightful change.

I believe the world will become a more productive and peaceful place when we all use the skill of listening.

This guide is a step towards that outcome.

Deep listening
does not require
elaborate
techniques,
tools or
high-tech devices.
It just *needs you*.

A common Thread

Mary arrives at work, greeted by a whole day of back-to-back meetings in her calendar. No time to have lunch, grab a refreshment or just pause and collect her thoughts. She is already frustrated and anxious and the day has barely begun.

As Mary approaches the first meeting room, her internal chatter is filling up the space in her mind. She fast-forwards to a high-stakes decision she needs to make by the end of the week.

Suddenly, her phone beeps, reminding her that she needs to pick up a friend from the airport tonight. What time does she need to leave work to make it? The traffic will be terrible because there is a storm predicted. What if the flight is delayed?

Mary is so lost in her own internal stories that she walks past the meeting room and has to turn back. She arrives just as Alice comes in announcing everyone is running 10 minutes late.

Everything is a blur in Mary's mind because she has been talking to herself incessantly. So she makes a commitment to give her complete and utter attention to the speaker for the next five minutes. As she does, the little monkey in her brain swings in with another idea and she realises that the communications update is due, so she makes a note of what to do on her phone.

Mary looks up and Peter is giving her a judgmental 'pay attention' kind of look. She looks at her watch, it's 15 minutes into the meeting, she hasn't been listening and now she feels frustrated, disappointed and annoyed.

Mary's mind continues to drift from the discussion, to the people in the room to the people outside the room, to the airport pick up tonight and an upcoming meeting with her manager. Before she has time to contribute, Mary excuses herself because she realises that she is now late for her next meeting.

She feels like a lab rat running from one meeting to the next without processing the last meeting, let alone getting ready for the next meeting.

Does this story sound extreme?

Or are you nodding along in familiarity?

I felt anxious writing this story, let alone reading it. This is an experience a client shared with me during a coaching meeting and it is a very common scenario that I hear from people at all levels of organisations.

The frantic pace that you are asked to perform at in your workplace creates a *productivity paradox* where we think more meetings, discussions and debates lead to higher quality discussion, decisions and impacts.

The opposite is true – fewer, but more focused meetings make a bigger impact.

The modern workplace creates so many *distractions* that we are too easily lost in our *own mind* before we are ready to start a *discussion* with someone else.

WHAT IS NOT LISTENING COSTING YOU?

1   If you are not present, and haven't really been listening, you can make the other person feel undervalued or even offend them.

2   Wasted time, as the conversation will no doubt occur many times again.

3   Confusion, conflict, lack of clarity, inability to learn from each other's experiences.

4 Jumping to conclusions that may be the wrong ones.

5 Misunderstandings, frustration, a sense of being isolated, no shared burdens or pain, relationships on hold, disappointments and increased fears.

6 I need to redo things, reprioritise tasks, lack of clarity, a lot of wasted cycles and time.

Lessons for listening

Intrinsically and intuitively we sense when people aren't listening. It might be the fact that they are looking away, looking at their watch or looking at their phone. Maybe they aren't letting you finish your sentences or their questions don't align to the dialogue.

Our gut instinct knows when others aren't listening because we are all natural born listeners. At 20 weeks in your mother's womb, you learned how to listen. You learned to listen before you learned how to breathe, before you learned to see or speak.

At 30 weeks, you could distinguish the sound of your mother from any other sound.

Humans are genetically coded to be deep and powerful listeners. It's vital to understand and hear where your mother is because it is essential to your survival.

Our ability to listen is not just one of our most critical skills; it is fundamental and essential to the survival of our species.

Yet from the moment you were born screaming to be heard, you forgot the skill of how to listen.

You were taught by your parents about why it's important to speak up. You were taught how to speak, but you were not taught how to listen.

This has carried throughout your adult life.

Only 2% of people are taught how to listen[2]. Congratulations if you are part of the 2%. For the other 98% of us, we must relearn what is our birth right – how to listen so that we can make an impact beyond just the words we hear.

---

2 http://www.listen.org/

You've been taught how to *speak,* but have you been taught how to *listen?*

WHAT IS NOT LISTENING COSTING YOU?

1 Guessing or assuming happens
and problems are not solved
or addressed.

2 The same issues keep occurring,
therefore people are blamed.

3 People get frustrated or upset
with each other

4   Disconnection, anxiety, fear, isolation and thinking no one understands me.

5   Missing vital information or getting the information wrong and even passing on the incorrect information.

6   People may not think I am interested, or not care as much as I do. They may think I do not value what they are saying.

Unconcsious listeners

We go our whole life without being taught how to listen. As a result, most of us fall into one of these four types of listeners:

1. Lost
2. Interrupting
3. Shrewd
4. Dramatic.

I'm sure you can think of people who listen in each of these ways when you are speaking. But what about when you are the listener? Which one are you guilty of?

1. The Lost Listener

You're in your own mind rather than in the conversation. You are so absorbed with your self-talk you don't create enough space for the dialogue to land in your mind, you are so busy thinking about your last thought or your next thought that you can't focus on the discussion. You are lost before you even turn up.

2. The Interrupting Listener

You are so focused on finding a solution to the problem that you finish the speaker's sentences for them. You feel they are moving too slowly in describing the issue, so you listen with the intent of solving, rather than their intent of being curious. You interrupt and interject, creating all kinds of confusion. You are busy solving problems the speaker hasn't yet verbalised.

3. The Shrewd Listener

You are too busy trying to solve the issue before listening to the explanation. You might be shrewd enough to wait patiently and not interrupt the speaker, but you are anticipating the future, trying to solve the problem before you've heard it or understood it all. You have forgotten to be present and to listen completely.

4. The Dramatic Listener

You love creating drama and exploring every element of the discussion. Rather than helping the speaker progress, you get stuck in the detail and dissecting the historical events and patterns that have led you to the discussion. You are so engrossed and engaged in the story that you become completely preoccupied in the theatre of the drama.

Discussions with these four types of listeners are *superficial* and lack impact. There is *another way*.

WHAT IS NOT LISTENING COSTING YOU?

1 Others can feel disrespected or belittled. You may miss key parts of the information or the underlying message. Does not demonstrate empathy.

2 Your own frame of reference and understandings is by nature, rather limiting. It would be a shame to live a life as limited as the one only you understand.

3 Poor listening leads to assumptions and misunderstanding.

4 Bad listeners make poor, boring conversation. Overall it just feels like a waste of time, so both parties end up displeased with the experience.

5 Others can feel disrespected or belittled. You may miss key parts of the information or the underlying message. Does not demonstrate empathy.

6 People will stop engaging in conversation with you as they will believe you are not interested in their opinion. You make assumptions.

Conscious listening

When we become conscious of how we listen, we begin to listen through the following perspectives:

1. Intentional
2. Systemic
3. Curious
4. Progressive.

Who do you admire for their listening skills? It's likely they demonstrate some of the following characteristics. Do you see some of your own listening strengths here?

1. Intentional Listening

You understand that listening is about what both parties bring to a conversation. Listening is a state of mind. Rather than just hearing words, sentences and stories you bring a presence to the discussion that creates space and opportunity to make a difference.

You understand the need to create the right state of mind for yourself before you commence the discussion. You help the speaker move into a productive state during the dialogue. You understand that your intention is the only thing that you can control in the dialogue.

2. Systemic Listening

You understand the bigger picture and that all people and problems are part of systems. You understand that systems are integrated and balanced. You listen to understand how the dialogue can be integrated and connected to other discussions, debates and situations.

In your mind and through your questions you can help the speaker expand the possibilities of their thinking in skilful and subtle ways. You create broader perspectives in the dialogue because you listen on a level others rarely explore.

3. Curious Listening

You love exploring the landscape of ideas and discussions. You are genuinely interested in the speaker and the discussion. You are a skilful and considered questioner. You understand that it's what's unsaid that is more powerful than the first thing out of the speaker's mouth.

Your curiosity and the skill of your questions help the speaker move out of their internal orientation and see the world from the outside.

4. Progressive Listening

Nothing makes you more excited than seeing the speaker arrive at a new insight through your discussions. You like starting the dialogue in one place, then leaving it in a more advanced state. Your outside perspective creates possibilities for them and the dialogue.

You create a sense of momentum and excitement in discussions. You want the speaker to leave the discussion more energised and optimistic. You are disciplined enough not to be fixated on how to get there. You are confident that the destination will reveal itself through progressing the discussion.

'Knowledge
speaks,
but wisdom
listens.'

JIMI HENDRIX

WHAT ARE THE BENEFITS OF DEEP LISTENING?

1 The listener is in a far better position to help the other person.

2 Listening enables learning and discovery. This can lead to new and more complete perspectives, which in turn mean better connections and decision making.

3 Seeing the full picture from someone's perspective and being able to absorb the full knowledge of the situation and know what you can help with.

4 For the speaker, they get a sense that they are valued. For the listener, they gain insight into how the other person is feeling and truly understanding what the problem is.

5 People who communicate to listen and understand experience have more stable and fulfilling relationships because their raw emotions, desires and issues are being heard, understood and actions are being taken as a result to improve their lives.

6 A true understanding of what is being said, and the ability to ask questions that will uncover unseen issues or challenges.

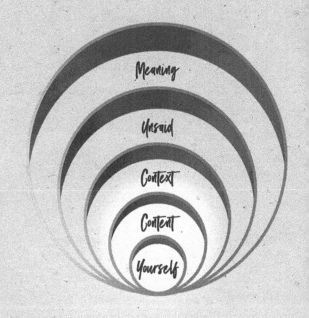

Meaning

Unsaid

Context

Content

Yourself

Five levels of listening

Most of us are good at hearing, but the difference between listening and hearing is that listening explores all the aspects of the dialogue, not just the words.

Traditional theories about listening centre on intention and attention to the other person, outlining techniques such as paraphrasing and active listening, which ensure all the attention is on the other person. This is useful, yet lacks impact.

I want to propose another approach, *beyond* the words, towards *listening* so you can *hear* what the other person *means*, rather than what they say.

There are five levels of listening that can help you become a deeper listener and create an impact rather than an impasse.

1. Listening to Yourself

Paradoxically, deep listening to others starts with listening to yourself first. You need time to tune in and recognise what is running through your own mind, then clear away this clutter and create a space to make room to hear others.

2. Listening to the Content

Once you have cleared the space in your own mind, you have more room to explore the landscape of the content. Listening to the speaker's words is critically important to those who are speaking, yet I think this only begins to scratch the surface of good listening. There are deeper and richer layers to explore. Content is a critical ingredient in the recipe of dialogue, but other ingredients are needed to make memorable and impactful outcomes.

3. Listening for the Context

The context is informed by the content. Asking thoughtful and provoking questions can help you clarify your understanding. These questions can help the other person explore a much broader context and landscape in their thinking. In turn, you both discover a richer range of alternatives. Some examples of clarifying questions include:

- What assumptions have you made to reach this conclusion?
- What would your customers or stakeholders say if they heard this discussion?
- Is this true in all circumstances?

4. Listening for the Unsaid

Dialogue is a simultaneous and fluid equation. Research shows that most people only speak at 125 words per minute, but their mind is processing at least 400 words per minute[3]. There is a considerable disconnect between what they want to say and what they are actually saying.

What's interesting to me is what you didn't say.

I have found this statement to be really powerful in helping someone else deepen their understanding of what they were thinking and discussing.

---

3 Factor Analysis of the Ability to Comprehend Time-Compressed Speech
Carver, Johnson, & Friedman, 1970

5. Listening for the Meaning

Content, context and the unsaid all contribute to the meaning. Meaning can be created for the person speaking, the person listening and collectively. Listening at the level of meaning helps us to make sense of the discussion and informs a wide range of perspectives and possibilities. It helps each party understand what has changed in their thinking since the conversation started.

Which level
do you
currently
listen at?

WHAT ARE THE BENEFITS OF DEEP LISTENING?

1   Clarity.

2   Making a connection with another person.

3   Learning new things about people, places and facts.

4   True communication. True understanding. True expression. True relatedness.

5   Learning something new.

6   Similar benefits to meditation. Joy from the connection with another.

The 125/400 rule

When it comes to deep listening, you must understand that there is a gap between what you hear and what your mind can process.

We speak between 125 and 175 words per minute, yet we can listen to 400 words per minute.

That means that no matter how fast they speak, your mind can process three to four times more words. It's this gap that causes you to drift off and be distracted.

So what usually happens with the time in between?

Our mind will drift or wander, and we'll often have the urge to interrupt midway through the conversation. This is something you need to be aware of. You need to stay in the discussion rather than somewhere else.

The reason why it's critical to pay attention and listen completely – including the pauses, the

silence and thoughtful moments in a discussion – is because of the simple maths between speaking and hearing. Remember, 125 words spoken yet 400 words can be heard. This is true for the speaker and this is true for the listener.

For any given thought that you might want to express you can only get out a quarter in spoken words for a given moment of time.

The likelihood that when speaking to you, the person can express the ideas in their mind completely and effectively the very first time they speak is four times lower than is possible.

In the pause, you and the speaker can completely and fully explore whatever is being discussed. The pause creates space for the speaker to fully express their idea with the remaining three quarters of the thinking in their own mind.

The speaker can also use the space created by the pause to revisit the way they just explained something in a more precise and succinct way or more complete way.

Either way, it will progress the discussion beyond where it started and creates a deeper and richer understanding for the listener and the speaker.

To be a deep listener and help your speaker progress their thinking, ask one of the following questions.

1. How long have you been thinking about this?

2. What else are you thinking about?

3. What's different about your thinking since we started discussing this?

4. What is it that you haven't said?

'Nothing *strengthens* authority so much as *silence*.'

LEONARDO DA VINCI

WHAT ARE THE BENEFITS OF DEEP LISTENING?

1 Avoiding misunderstanding.

2 True engagement with others; a sense of connection.

3 Positive relationships, whether work or personal.

4 Faster and more efficient outcomes.

5 Emotional connection and information/knowledge sharing.

6 Empathy.

Clear the clutter

Great dialogue is like the ebb and flow of the waves on a beach. There is a natural tempo and movement between the water and the sand.

Done well, it is an easy and effortless interaction between two people. Occasionally, like a poorly formed wave, a conversation can come crashing down around you – messy and wasteful.

So what's the trick to an effortless flow?

You must listen deeply to yourself before you start the process of listening to others.

Before you engage in dialogue, you need to start from a quiet place within yourself.

Recognise what is running through your own mind and then clear away this clutter to make room to hear the other person.

If you and your self-talk are in deep discussion (like Mary in Chapter 1 – A Common Thread), it's difficult for you to be available to listen.

Your self-talk will immediately distract from your ability to listen and understand – ultimately detracting from your ability to make an impact.

WHAT MAKES A GREAT LISTENER?

1 Focus on what is being said, with eye contact, empathy and nodding to demonstrate you are listening. Provide physical signals that you are listening, not just 'hearing', what is being said. Repeat back or 'clarify' what has been said to confirm accuracy of details.

2 Giving one's undivided attention to that person, reacting to their words with a yes or a nod or a smile from time to time, or asking the odd question for clarification if necessary.

3 Allowing the other person to speak and not interrupting. People often need to show their intelligence or knowledge and so they interrupt. A good listener is someone who used prompts at the right moments to encourage the other person to share further.

4 Someone who doesn't interrupt. Someone who can keep their mind still. Someone who also asks the right questions to understand the issue deeper.

5 Someone who is 'present' and helps you discover a deeper place of what you're trying to say or think, by asking 'generously curious' questions. They also leave space, and delight in it.

6 A good listener is someone who used prompts at the right moments to encourage the other person to share further.

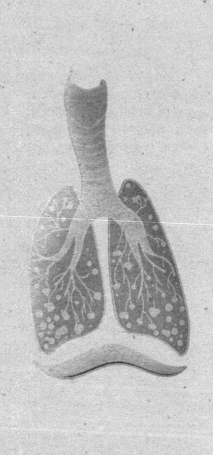

Breathe

Zazen, from the practice of Zen, is a deep reflection and meditation on the role of the breath to regulate the mind through focus.

Yogis call this deep breathing practice *Paranayama*, or the breath of life.

Modern neuroscience reinforces the importance of breathing on the brain's ability to allow the mind to relax, expand and listen, with Dr Herbert Benson[4] explaining how breathing helps control the parasympathetic nervous system and counter the fight or flight responses to modern day distraction and stress.

---

4 *The Relaxation Response* by Herbert Benson 2000

Whether we view the world through the teachings of the many centuries and cultures or through modern neuroscience, the conclusion is the same – our breathing and our listening are closely connected.

It almost sounds too simple and easy to be true, but to listen deeply you have to listen to your breathing.

Try it now.

Notice the speed and depth of your breathing. What can you do to slow it down? What can you do to deepen it and hold it a little longer?

This act of slowing your breath automatically creates a space in your mind where you can listen to yourself more deliberately. This is great to practice when you're preparing for the next meeting, phone call or conversation with someone.

The practice of listening is closely connected to the rhythm of your breathing. When you get this, then you start to understand how to listen deeply.

Being a natural deep listener is as natural as being a great breather. Throughout life, we just haven't been encouraged to recognise this.

Deep listening requires connecting with your breathing, your body and your mind. You need to unlearn what you've learned to become a deep and powerful listener.

The deeper you're *breathing,* the deeper you're *listening.*

WHAT MAKES A GREAT LISTENER?

1   Shows focus and pays attention to what you are saying.

2   The combination of creating the environment, safety and space for someone to speak, together with the presence and engagement of the listener so that the speaker feels heard.

3   The ability to tune out inner thoughts and avoid the temptation to plan a response before the other person has finished speaking.

4 They pay full attention to what is being said, and provide physical and verbal feedback to show they are listening. They internalise and understand/ playback meaning to them.

5 Care, curiosity and a genuine interest in others. The ability to shut up.

6 Asks questions based on what you have said.

Create space

Silence is the tuning fork for your listening ear.

Your ability to listen beyond noise for signals will tune your hearing ear to the ideal frequency. This is a function of how much space you can explore and contrast with the noise around you.

A simple way to increase silence is to close your eyes for 15 seconds before a conversation, phone call or meeting.

If you are uncomfortable with closing your eyes, you can simply place your head in your hands to close out the light and help reduce the noise in your own mind.

When you create space in your own mind, you allow space for the conversation to land and expand without competition or judgment.

The space you create in your mind from just 15 seconds of silence will significantly improve your ability to listen and take in information.

You can modify this exercise so you are sitting, standing or walking between meetings with your eyes open.

TRY NOW

1. Sit upright with your back firmly in the chair
2. Place both feet on the ground
3. Place both your hands in your lap
4. Close your eyes
5. Take a long, deep and complete inhalation
6. Hold this breath for a few seconds
7. Exhale slowly and deeply for twice as long as you would normally
8. Repeat for 15 breaths
9. Visualise your breath moving in and out of your body
10. Open your eyes.

How much more clear-headed and open to listening do you feel?

Caring and
respecting
the pause
is the step in
fully listening
to what
is unsaid.

WHAT MAKES A GREAT LISTENER?

1 They don't take the focus of
the conversation in their direction
unless it is directly relevant
and beneficial.

2 They are not judgmental.

3 Someone empathetic, who
tries to understand your point
of view, and doesn't butt in.
Someone who actually considers
what you're saying before
responding. Someone open, but
gentle. Someone who seeks to
understand rather than just listen.

4 Someone who is not distracted
by the world around them,
and is instead tuned into
what you are saying.

5 They do not allow preconceived
ideas/feelings cloud their
interaction. They are willing to
learn. They accept and admit to
when they are wrong and are
willing to listen to constructive
feedback. They are enthusiastic,
have positive body language, and
are willing to take the appropriate
time dependant on the situation.

6 Someone who is present
and open to connection.

Mind the gap

Another ingredient for deep listening is to treat a pause like it's another word in the conversation.

The likelihood that someone can express an idea in their head completely, fully and effectively the very first time they speak it is very low. (The 125/400 Rule in Chapter 5 explains and proves this.)

Therefore, it's critical to understand that the pause, the silence, the breath – that moment when the speaker revisits what they haven't fully expressed – isn't the time for you to jump in and ask a question that will help contrast your perspective or create a new path in the discussion.

Their pause is the most critical moment in your listening.

It is in the pause where you start to notice what someone's intention is. A pause moves the speaker from a place of thinking you are listening to a place where they feel *heard*.

The pause is usually the gap between words and thoughts. Silence is the space where the speaker becomes reflective and revisits what they have said to see if they have fully explored the space in their mind for all their ideas and connections.

A pause is a breath and silence is a thought. Both must be treated with the devotion as any fully formed and spoken word.

When you understand the importance of honouring silence, space and pause in a discussion, you start to explore the world beyond words.

There are
many other
dimensions
to listening
rather than
just hearing
what is
being spoken.

WHAT MAKES A GREAT LISTENING ENVIRONMENT?

1 No other distractions, e.g. mobile phones, laptops, TV.

2 Free of distractions and loud noises.

3 When people put away their phones, not having slide decks, when people know their roles is to contribute.

4 An environment that is inviting
without too many distractions.

5 Trust between all parties.
No judgment. Safe place to listen
and speak your mind.

6 Ensuring that one person
at a time speaks; that everyone
is to share an opinion; a 10
second silence after each speaker
to allow reflections.

Beyond words

So much of the literature about listening commences with the theory that the *speaker* – not the *listener* – is the most important person in the conversation. I take the opposite view.

The speaker is NOT the most important person in the conversation.

Conversation is a dialogue of equals. For the dialogue to be successful both parties need to play a role rather than one person being subjugated to the position of an active listener.

A listener who is only focused on the words is listening at a superficial level and the depth of the conversation will be shallow and the impact limited. We need to listen beyond words to understand the essence of what is being said and what is unspoken.

Listening at the level of words is essential only when you understand *it's not the only level you need to listen on.*

Think of it like you're enjoying a wonderful meal. To start, you're usually presented with a menu. Each dish on the menu has a recipe and each recipe has ingredients. Words are the ingredients to a wonderful meal. Ingredients alone don't create the meal. A wonderful meal is a combination of dishes over time – entrée, main and dessert.

Words are the ingredients of a great conversation, but you need a recipe to make sense of all the words.

Understanding the words is where most listening and communication books start and, unfortunately, where most of them end.

Techniques like active listening, paraphrasing, summarising, verbal confirmation, and body mirroring are great places to start learning to listen – they are just the beginning rather than the end of the practice of listening.

Listening to the context of what is being said is a critical step in moving from being solely focused on the words to being focused on the dialogue. It moves your listening away from your own ego and the ego of the other person towards understanding what the dialogue has to offer both people in conversation and, more importantly, what the dialogue has to offer others outside the discussion.

Ken Wilber's work in the 1970s sought to create an approach to help people understand what context they were currently operating from, what context needs to be more fully explored and what context would serve the conversation best.

Wilber's Integral Theory is an approach to unifying Eastern and Western thinking and philosophies. His Integral Model presents four orientations of context. This becomes a simple navigational tool to explore dialogue four times more effectively, because it creates a way to fully listen to the 400 words that are unsaid by the speaker.

The four dimensions of the model help you listen through a different perspective to understand a different context each time.

The four perspectives are:

1. Internal

– is the discussion focused inside their system or organisation?

2. External

– is the discussion focused outside their system or organisation?

3. Individual

– is the discussion focused on them?

4. Collective

– is the discussion focused beyond them?

The Integral Model assists you as the listener in creating another opportunity to navigate skilfully through each dimension, which elegantly maps the missing words from the 125/400 Rule. It provides four additional perspectives for you to listen to when your mind starts to wander.

'One hour of compassionate *deep listening* can bring about transformation and *healing*.'

THICH NHAT HANH

WHAT MAKES A GREAT LISTENING ENVIRONMENT?

1 High value placed on communication/feedback, space for everyone to be heard, minimal distractions, productive dialogue.

2 The ability to speak without fear.

3 Ground rules with an environment conducive to listening and feeling safe.

4 When people find the courage
to have a courageous conversation.
When people go out on a limb to
have a real conversation others
often reciprocate.

5 Common interest. Proper group
structures. Understanding roles.

6 Engagement – get people involved
by either asking them questions
or getting them to contribute.

Unsaid

Listening on a deeper level takes great discipline and patience.

Deep listeners who transform everyone's thinking are listening for the gaps – what's absent and what's *not being said*.

Deep listeners are engaged in the process of not just connecting words, phrases and sentences, they are listening beyond the obvious. They connect the patterns, the common links in stories and ultimately, they are searching for *meaning* rather than *understanding*.

Listening for what's **said** is like spending all your time looking at the sun and saying that because the sun is the most obvious and brightest part of the sky, it is the only star in the solar system.

Listening for what's **unsaid** is about taking a broader perspective – it's about taking an explorer mindset to looking at the solar system and first noticing the sky, the clouds and the sun before we explore Mars, Jupiter and beyond.

Are you spending too much of your time in the obvious place listening to what is being said?

As you've explored, you speak at 125 words per minute and your mind can process 400 words per minute. The simplest way to close the gap between the two during a dialogue is by regularly exploring the space between what the speaker wants to say and what they actually said.

It is three times more impactful to explore what hasn't been said in the discussion.

The best way to do this is to ask your speaker what else they want to say, but haven't already.

What's interesting to me is what you didn't say?

'The most *important* thing in *communication* is hearing *what isn't said.*'

PETER DRUCKER

WHAT MAKES A GREAT LISTENING ENVIRONMENT?

1 When people care about what is being said to each other and pay attention.

2 One that is more concerned about hearing everyone's opinions and ideas or reflections on what was said.

3 Calm, quiet and clean.

4 A calm room without distractions, a group who have different experiences and thoughts.

5 A facilitator/leader who clarifies values, behaviours and intention of the group, frames the expectations, and models them.

6 Also, coffee ;-)

Dig deep foundations

Deep listening is a practice – a process that needs to be constantly improved and refined over time. This means it requires a solid foundation.

Consider the foundations of a building.

When creating the foundation, large holes are made in the ground for the concrete to be poured into. Yet the process of adding concrete alone is inherently unstable without the steel reinforcement. It's the combination of the deep holes, concrete and steel that gives a building the ability to withstand great winds and earthquakes.

Now think about this as the foundation for listening.

The deep excavation holes are the space you create in your mind to receive the conversation from the other person. This structure is unstable because you will become distracted during the discussion as the words pour in.

It's your ability to notice when you are distracted and quickly reset your thinking, or to avoid the urge of jumping into the conversation too early that is the steel of listening. Breathing, silence and space in your mind work together to create powerful and impactful conversations.

The success of any conversation is created well before the other person is present in the discussion. It's a mathematical certainty – through the 125/400 Rule – that you will drift off in a discussion even if you are the most amazing listener.

The journey to becoming the great listener you were born to be means taking a little bit more time to dig this deep foundation for listening.

It would be incredibly short term to think that everything about listening is about hearing and the external conversation.

Listening happens before hearing commences.

Deep listening creates
life-changing
opportunities.

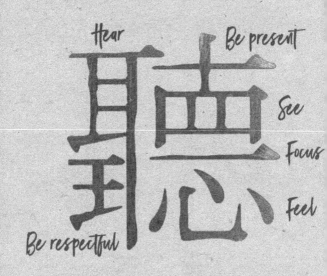

Ancient wisdom

There is a simple holistic tool that has been around for thousands of years that you can use to integrate your understanding of listening. It is the Chinese character called 'Ting', which explains the term 'To Listen'.

Only two elements of Ting deal with the body – Hear and See. The other four elements of Ting deal with your emotions and state of mind.

1. Presence

Being present is about what you do before and during the conversation. Preparing yourself by listening to yourself in advance of the conversation will make you more present during the discussion. Clearing space in your mind to hear makes your ears more available to listen.

2. Respect

The context of respect in Ting is about having as much reverence for the conversation as if you were speaking to royalty. This is the space to fully explore not just the words, but also the silence and what is unsaid.

3. Focus

Focus is about what you do when you inevitably get distracted or confused by what you are hearing. Focus is the speed at which you return to the conversation with your complete attention on the discussion as well as on the speaker, despite the distractions.

4. Feel

When you listen with your heart, you remove judgment from the discussion and bring empathy to the space. In feeling your way through a conversation, you also bring compassion and care for the person, their situation and the dialogue.

5. Hear

As you fully engage your ears, you start to deliberately focus on the discussion, and not on the people or situation outside of the conversation. You may become distracted, but it's your ability to refocus on the conversation when you are distracted that's vital to hearing.

6. See

Our sight is the natural counter-balance to our hearing. Both are useful, yet used together they are powerful. Our sight helps align words with body movements and hand gestures. It's human instinct to notice when the words are incongruent. If we are operating at a conscious level in our listening, we not only feel, we also notice the incongruence between the spoken word and the visual image that accompanies it.

Ting is your gut feel – it's your gut that notices without any training when people aren't listening completely. Trust your gut.

Ting teaches us many things including balance between our body and mind during listening. It also teaches us the multi-dimensional nature of listening.

The balanced elements of Ting create richness in listening, and in their depth they create power. With this power comes impact for the speaker and the listener, and ultimately the dialogue.

Put-Ting
into *practice*
Be present,
respectful,
and feel,
focus, see
and hear what
is *being said*.

Closing Thoughts

The ancient Aboriginal people's practice of *Dadirri* is based on inner quiet, silent awareness, a place of stillness and contemplation about the individual first and then their connection to the outside world. This practice commenced 40,000 years ago and continues today through the teachings of Aboriginal Elders.

Dadirri is about your connection to the lands in which you inhabit. It's about deeply listening to what the lands are saying back to you, because you belong to the lands. Dadirri is about your connection to community and how you listen deeply to others.

The practice of Dadirri is about listening to your community through silence.

This is how we enact real change in the world.

Listening is complex and nuanced. It's situational as well as relational. It's not just about what you hear. It's not just about what you see. It's much more than that.

It's about respect.

So let's reflect on your conversations right now.

1. How respectful are you right now
    in conversation?
2. Are you racing to get your point across,
    to be seen as the expert?
3. Or are you embracing the silence and
    exploring possibilities?

It is through listening that you can be the change
you want to see in others.

It is the questions that bring answers, not the
statements that create impact.

'We do not *grow* by knowing all of the *answers*, but rather by *living* with the *questions*.'

MAX DE PREE

RESOURCES

LISTENING

Five ways to listen better – Julian Treasure, TedTalk

How to truly listen – Evelyn Glennie, TedTalk

Listen: Nature is quieter than ever before – Jennifer S. Holland, National Geographic

READING

What great listeners actually do– Zenger and Folkman, *Harvard Business Review*

Listening to people – Nichols and Stevens, *Harvard Business Review*

The discipline of listening – Ram Charan, *Harvard Business Review*

Why listening is so much more than hearing – Seth Horowitz, *The New York Times*

I am listening

I am passionate about using the gift of listening to bring positive change in homes, workplaces and the world. If you would like to speak to me, I am here to listen.

These are the best ways to stay in contact or learn more about becoming a deep listener.

Find out more about the available Deep Listening programs and keynote presentations: **oscartrimboli.com/speaks**

Keynote Speaking

Raise the consciousness of your audience and motivate them to understand the impact their listening can have on themselves and others. Delivered to your organisation, annual kick-off events or to your people manager community. You'll get simple and actionable steps to become a more impactful listener.

Deep Listening Programs

For in-house groups who want to understand the foundational elements of deep listening. For teams, people managers and executives, who need to deliver on transformational change or significant projects. These workshops are designed to ensure you learn to listen deeply.

My blog

Keep up to date with tips, tools and techniques on how to listen deeply, as well as announcements for upcoming events.
oscartrimboli.com/blog

The Apple Award-Winning Podcast — Deep Listening

Move yourself from an unconscious listener to deep and impactful listener by following the tips through the five levels of listening.
oscartrimboli.com/podcast

Deep Listening Community

Join our active community on Facebook. There you can listen and learn from others about practical ways to improve your listening.
oscartrimboli.com/facebook

Most importantly...

Don't forget to call or connect:

+61 410 340 185
hello@oscartrimboli.com
oscartrimboli.com

About

OSCAR TRIMBOLI is an author, Host of the Apple Award winning podcast—Deep Listening and a sought after keynote speaker. He is passionate about using the gift of listening to bring positive change in homes, workplaces and the world.

Through his work with chairs, boards of directors and executive teams in local, regional and global organisations, Oscar has experienced firsthand the transformational impact leaders and organisations can have when they listen beyond the words.

He believes that leadership teams need to focus their attention and their listening on building organisations that have impact and create powerful legacies for the the people they serve – today and, more importantly, for future generations.

Oscar is a marketing and technology industry veteran with over 30 years' experience across general management, sales, marketing and operations for Microsoft, PeopleSoft, Polycom, Professional Advantage and Vodafone.

During his time as a marketing director at Microsoft, he was accountable for the five-year journey to move Microsoft Office from DVDs to the Data Centre.

He consults to organisations including 20th Century Fox, AstraZeneca, BAE Systems, CBRE, Cisco, Commonwealth Bank, Energy Australia, Google, HSBC, IAG, Macquarie University, PayPal, Qantas, Reebok, SAP, TAL, Thomson Reuters, TripAdvisor and Universal Music.

Oscar lives in Sydney with his wife Jennie, where he helps first-time runners and ocean swimmers conquer their fears and contributes to the cure for cancer as part of Can Too, a cancer research charity – **cantoo.org.au**

For more about
Oscar's Deep
Listening Programs
for individuals,
teams
and organisations:

+61 410 340 185
oscartrimboli.com

Printed in December 2021
by Rotomail Italia S.p.A., Vignate (MI) - Italy